TCHAIKOVSKY'S THE NUTCRACKER

ALTO SAX

Arranged and Recorded by Donald Sosin

Cherry Lane Music Company
Educational Director/Project Supervisor: Susan Poliniak
Director of Publications: Mark Phillips
Manager of Publications Gabrielle Fastman

ISBN-13: 978-1-57560-968-3
ISBN-10: 1-57560-968-1

Visit our website at www.cherrylane.com

OVERTURE

By Pyotr Il'yich Tchaikovsky

TRACK 1

ALTO SAX

MARCH

By Pyotr Il'yich Tchaikovsky

ALTO SAX

SPANISH DANCE

("Chocolate")

By Pyotr Il'yich Tchaikovsky

ALTO SAX

ARABIAN DANCE
("Coffee")

By Pyotr Il'yich Tchaikovsky

TRACK 4

ALTO SAX

CHINESE DANCE
("Tea")

By Pyotr Il'yich Tchaikovsky

ALTO SAX

RUSSIAN DANCE
(Trepak)

By Pyotr Il'yich Tchaikovsky

TRACK 6

ALTO SAX

Molto vivace ♩ = 128

DANCE OF THE REED FLUTES

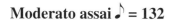

By Pyotr Il'yich Tchaikovsky

ALTO SAX

Moderato assai ♪ = 132

WALTZ OF THE FLOWERS

By Pyotr Il'yich Tchaikovsky

ALTO SAX

DANCE OF THE SUGARPLUM FAIRY

TRACK 9

By Pyotr Il'yich Tchaikovsky

ALTO SAX

FINAL WALTZ AND APOTHEOSIS

By Pyotr Il'yich Tchaikovsky

ALTO SAX

Coda

great songs series

Cherry Lane Music is proud to present this legendary series which has delighted players and performers for generations.

Great Songs of the Fifties

The latest release in Cherry Lane's acclaimed Great Songs series, this songbook presents 51 musical memories from the fabulous '50s! Features rock, pop, country, Broadway and movie tunes, including: All Shook Up • At the Hop • Blue Suede Shoes • Dream Lover • Fly Me to the Moon • Kansas City • Love Me Tender • Misty • Peggy Sue • Rock Around the Clock • Sea of Love • Sixteen Tons • Take the "A" Train • Wonderful! Wonderful! • and more. Includes an introduction by award-winning journalist Bruce Pollock.

_____02500323 P/V/G.............................$16.95

Great Songs of the Sixties, Vol. 1 – Revised Edition

The newly updated version of this classic book includes 80 faves from the 1960s: Angel of the Morning • Bridge over Troubled Water • Cabaret • Different Drum • Do You Believe in Magic • Eve of Destruction • Georgy Girl • It Was a Very Good Year • Monday, Monday • People • Spinning Wheel • Walk on By • and more.

_____02509902 P/V/G.............................$19.95

Great Songs of the Sixties, Vol. 2 – Revised Edition

61 more 60s hits: And When I Die • California Dreamin' • Crying • The 59th Street Bridge Song (Feelin' Groovy) • For Once in My Life • Honey • Little Green Apples • MacArthur Park • Me and Bobby McGee • Nowhere Man • Piece of My Heart • Sugar, Sugar • You Made Me So Very Happy • and more.

_____02509904 P/V/G.............................$19.95

Great Songs of the Seventies – Revised Edition

This super collection of 70 big hits from the '70s includes: After the Love Has Gone • Afternoon Delight • Annie's Song • Band on the Run • Cold as Ice • FM • Imagine • It's Too Late • Layla • Let It Be • Maggie May • Piano Man • Shelter from the Storm • Superstar • Sweet Baby James • Time in a Bottle • The Way We Were • more!

_____02509917 P/V/G.............................$19.95

Prices, contents, and availability subject to change without notice.

Great Songs of the Seventies – Volume 2

Features 58 outstanding '70s songs in rock, pop, country, Broadway and movie genres: American Woman • Baby, I'm-A Want You • Day by Day • Do That to Me One More Time • Dog & Butterfly • Don't Cry Out Loud • Dreamboat Annie • Follow Me • Get Closer • Grease • Heard It in a Love Song • I'll Be There • It's a Heartache • The Loco-Motion • My Eyes Adored You • New Kid in Town • Night Fever • On and On • Sing • Summer Breeze • Tonight's the Night • We Are the Champions • Y.M.C.A. • and more. Includes articles by Cherry Lane Music Company founder Milt Okun, and award-winning music journalist Bruce Pollock.

_____02500322 P/V/G.............................$19.95

Great Songs of the Eighties – Revised Edition

This newly revised edition features 50 songs in rock, pop & country styles, plus hits from Broadway and the movies! Songs: Almost Paradise • Angel of the Morning • Do You Really Want to Hurt Me • Endless Love • Flashdance...What a Feeling • Guilty • Hungry Eyes • (Just Like) Starting Over • Let Love Rule • Missing You • Patience • Through the Years • Time After Time • Total Eclipse of the Heart • and more.

_____02502125 P/V/G.............................$18.95

Great Songs of the Nineties

This terrific collection features 48 big hits in many styles. Includes: Achy Breaky Heart • Beautiful in My Eyes • Believe • Black Hole Sun • Black Velvet • Blaze of Glory • Building a Mystery • Crash into Me • Fields of Gold • From a Distance • Glycerine • Here and Now • Hold My Hand • I'll Make Love to You • Ironic • Linger • My Heart Will Go On • Waterfalls • Wonderwall • and more.

_____02500040 P/V/G.............................$16.95

Great Songs of the Pop Era

Over 50 hits from the pop era, including: Amazed • Annie's Song • Ebony and Ivory • Every Breath You Take • Hey Nineteen • I Want to Know What Love Is • I'm Every Woman • Just the Two of Us • Leaving on a Jet Plane • My Cherie Amour • Raindrops Keep Fallin' on My Head • Rocky Mountain High • This Is the Moment • Time After Time • (I've Had) the Time of My Life • What a Wonderful World and more!

_____02500043 Easy Piano.....................$16.95

CHERRY LANE MUSIC COMPANY

6 East 32nd Street, New York, NY 10016

Quality in Printed Music

Visit Cherry Lane on the Internet at
www.cherrylane.com

EXCLUSIVELY DISTRIBUTED BY

HAL•LEONARD® CORPORATION

7777 W. BLUEMOUND RD. P.O. BOX 13819 MILWAUKEE, WI 53213

0402